Jewish Roots: 101

Jewish Roots: 101
An Introduction

Jeffrey D. Johnson, PhD

www.israeltodayministries.org
www.Facebook.com/IsraelTodayMinistries
Galileeman@juno.com

JEWISH ROOTS 101
An Introduction

Copyright © 2017 Jeffrey D. Johnson. All rights reserved. Except for brief quotations in critical publications or reviews, no part of this book may be reproduced in any manner without prior written permission from the publisher. Write: Permissions, Wipf and Stock Publishers, 199 W. 8th Ave., Suite 3, Eugene, OR 97401.

Wipf & Stock
An Imprint of Wipf and Stock Publishers
199 W. 8th Ave., Suite 3
Eugene, OR 97401

www.wipfandstock.com

PAPERBACK ISBN: 978-1-5326-1945-8
HARDCOVER ISBN: 978-1-4982-4571-5

Manufactured in the U.S.A. APRIL 19, 2017

Contents

Christianity — The Beginning 7
Hebrew Bible 8
Rejoicing in the Law (Torah) 9
Education 9
Marcion: Archenemy of the "Jew God" 12
Jewish Connection Severed 13
Wrath vs Love 13
The Church: Guilty 14
Jewish Connection Revisited 14
A Jewish Framework 19
Christianity is Jewish 19
500 Synagogues 20
Canon 20
Heritage 23
Worship 24
Jewish Roots 24
Bibliography 27
About the Author 31

Christianity — The Beginning

To understand who we are as Christians is to understand our beginning. Did Jesus intend to have His "Church" separated from the Jewish community? Did the Apostle Paul emphasize a truncation of the Jewish cradle for this new community of unique people? What does the New Testament teach about Jesus, His followers and the new sect He founded? Did the Church replace Israel? Do Gentile Christians need to worship in a Jewish form? Who was this man called Jesus, and what were the influences in His life?

The church in the 21st century would do itself a disservice to not acknowledge its Jewish beginnings or to ignore the man Jesus and the cultural mores that shaped His teaching.

Christian communities throughout the world generally are relevant within their cultural construct. How are Christians to worship, and what does emulating Jesus mean? Form and freedom of worship is the goal. The freedom to worship in a form that is relevant and understandable, a form that is honoring to God and scripturally sound, is the emphasis you will find in the New Testament.

To diminish the significance of the Jewish roots of Christianity is an error. To read the Scripture realizing the Middle Eastern influence of the text, to understand Christianity's Jewish beginning, and to emulate Jesus's spirituality are goals for the Christian experience. The church must never forget the cradle from which it came! To mirror the religion Jesus founded is to understand the culture and religion of Israel.

"But as for you, continue in what you have learned and have become convinced of, because you know those from whom you learned it, and how from infancy you have known the holy Scriptures, which are able to make you wise for salvation through faith in Christ Jesus" (2 Tim. 3:14, 15 NIV).

Hebrew Bible

The Apostle Paul reminded Timothy to remember what he had learned and from whom he learned spiritual things. The cornerstone and foundation upon which Christianity and the New Testament rests is the Jewish Bible, commonly called the Old Testament. Jewish people refer to the Old Testament as the "Hebrew Bible" or "Tenach" (also spelled Tenakh or Tanak). The foundation upon which New Testament faith rests securely is the Hebrew Bible.[1]

There are no vowels in the Hebrew language, only vowel sounds, therefore the word Tenach is derived from three consonants:

---

1 Marvin R. Wilson, *Our Father Abraham: Jewish Roots of the Christian Faith* (Grand Rapids: Eerdmans Publishing Co., 1989), 107

1. T (Tav, ת) – Torah – means: teaching, direction or the way
2. N (Nun, נ) – Nevi'im – Prophets
3. K (Khaf, כ) – Ketuvim – Writings

Rejoicing in the Law (Torah)

Religious Jewish people love the Tenach. Every year in the Synagogue, the Torah is read completely. At the conclusion of the reading is a celebration called "Simchat Torah" that usually falls in the months of September or October. During this celebration the Torah scrolls are carried around the sanctuary. People praise God and rejoice in the teaching of the Law.

Simchat Torah means "Rejoicing in the Torah" which marks the end of the reading cycle and the beginning of the new.

Education

Love for the Scripture was quite evident with the followers of Jesus. Education was highly esteemed and valued in Jewish society. Josephus stated: *"Above all we pride ourselves on the education of our children, and regard as the most essential task in life the observance of our laws and of the pious practices based thereupon, which we have inherited."* –Against Apion, 60

The Babylonian Talmud, Shabbat 30a states: *"Study is one of the highest forms of worship."*

The Mishnah, Avot 2:12 states: *"Discipline yourself to study Torah, for you do not acquire it by inheritance."*

These texts remind us of the Jews at Berea who *"Were more noble...and searched the scriptures daily, whether those things were so"* (Acts 17:11 KJV).

These sayings were probably the motivational impetus behind Paul's statement: *"Study to shew thyself approved unto God, a workman that needeth not to be ashamed, rightly dividing the Word of truth"* (2 Tim. 2:15 KJV; cf. 2 Tim. 3:14-16; Heb. 4:12).

Peter declared: *"Giving all diligence, add to your faith, virtue, and to virtue knowledge"* (2 Pet. 1:5 KJV).

Peter also stated, *"Having been born again, not of corruptible seed but incorruptible, through the word of God which lives and abides forever."* Jesus said, *"Sanctify them by Your truth, Your word is truth"* (1 Pet. 1:23 and John 17:17 NKJV).

The New Testament was in the process of being written. So to what direct reference were Paul, Peter and Jesus referring to? The Old Testament Scriptures, the Tenach or Hebrew Scriptures! It is indeed inappropriate when the church deprecates the significance of the first 39 books of the Bible. Perhaps we should call the Old Testament by a better name, such as the First or Original Testament. We never read anywhere in the New Testament that the first 39 books of

Scripture were ever referred to as "Old" or abolished. It is the chief source from which our common Judeo-Christian heritage derives.[2]

It was certainly an unfortunate day for the Church when the Jewish Scriptures began to be called the "Old Testament" implying that this testament is now passé.[3] Jesus, nor the apostles, never declared the first 39 books of sacred Scripture dead or abolished. Therefore, they must never become so for the Church.[4]

The value of the Tenach in terms of biblical studies and theology can scarcely be overestimated. In *Ethics in a Permissive Society*, William Barclay said, "The Old Testament is the parent of the New Testament and the religion of the Old Testament is the cradle from which Christianity came."[5]

The church has to struggle against a rationalistic culture, and a spirituality steeped completely in idealism and mysticism [that] the normal path to a genuine understanding of the New Testament is by way of the Old. For in the Old Testament we come upon a world completely unaffected by the whole Hellenic spirit.[6]

---

2   Ibid.

3   Ibid.

4   Ibid.

5   William Barclay, *Ethics in a Permissive Society* (New York: Harper & Row, 1971), 13-14

6   Emil Brunner, "The Significance of the Old Testament for our Faith," *The Old Testament & Christian Faith: A Theological Discussion,* ed. Bernhard W. Anderson, (New York: Herder & Herder, 1969), 242

A thorough knowledge of the Old Testament is imperative if we are to grasp the Hebraic foundation which underpins the theology and life of the early Church. Most Christians have come to believe that the Old Testament is boring and irrelevant. This kind of reaction can be traced, at least in part, to the curricula or lack of curricula at Christian colleges and theological seminaries.

Marcion: Archenemy of the "Jew God"

The strains of a deeper dynamic are at work, an historical cancer that may be traced to Marcion in the second century. Following the New Testament era, one of the first heresies that the church faced was propounded by Marcion, a wealthy ship owner in Turkey who came to Rome in AD 138. He began to argue that the Old Testament was inferior to the New and had no part of authoritative revelation. He fought to have it removed from the canon. To some degree, Marcion appears to have been influenced by the dualistic teachings of Gnosticism and Platonism. Marcion's goal was to rid Christianity of every trace of Judaism. He became known as the archenemy of the "Jew God" and eventually was excommunicated.[7]

Unfortunately, Marcion's influence is still felt today almost 2,000 years later. In our concerted effort to be New Testament believers, we have too often unconsciously minimized

---

7   Wilson, *Our Father Abraham*, 108-109

the place and importance of the Old Testament and historic Hebrew roots.

Jewish Connection Severed

Today, Neo-Marcionism is a vanguard in promulgating the false teaching that Israel has been permanently cast aside and has no theological significance in today's world. Unfortunately, there are popular movements within protestant denominations that embrace this point of view. The fruit of this teaching is found in the deprecation of the reading of the Old Testament among Christians and the emphasis of Hellenistic interpretation of the Scripture from the pulpit. Yes, Christianity was cradled in a Hellenistic culture; however, the religion from which it came was Hebraic. Therefore, looking into the Hebrew construct is where one begins to understand the Christian faith and the faith of Jesus, not the Hellenistic.

Wrath vs Love

People hear comparisons like: The Book of Wrath vs the Book of Love; Law to Gospel; The New Testament has superseded the Old; the New Testament is better than the Old; The Old came before the Cross. The Church has been led to believe the Old Testament has no relevance today. And yet, when we read in the New Testament of the significance of the Word, the writers were referring to the Old Testament, since the New Testament was being written and would not be canonized or ratified until the third Council of Carthage (AD 397).

The Church: Guilty

The Church has been guilty of overemphasizing the dissimilarities of the Testaments. It has stressed the antithetical relationship of the Testaments rather than their continuity. This problem is very old and can be traced back to the increasing influence of the Greek culture and non-Jewish thought, contrast and contradiction, rather than an acknowledgement of roots.[8]

Jewish Connection Revisited

What are some of the historical footnotes that we need to understand in order to reverse this unfortunate negative emphasis in the 21st century?

1. If we are to emulate Jesus, then we must understand Him in the context of 1st century Judaism and how He interpreted and understood the Tenach, or the first 39 books of Scripture.

2. Jesus was Jewish. He was born under the Law and as a Jew was instructed in the Torah (Gal. 4:4).[9]

---

8   Abraham J. Heschel, *The Insecurity of Freedom* (New York: Schocken Books, 1972), 169

9   Eugene J. Fisher, *Faith Without Prejudice* (New York: Paulist Press, 1977), 33

3. Mary and Joseph were religious Jews who observed the commandments of the Jewish faith in raising Jesus according to Matthew 1 and Luke 2.

4. Jesus would have been included in the covenant with Abraham and made a member of the Jewish community and faith through circumcision (Luke 2:21-24).

   Verses 22-24 record for us two points of Jewish law:

   a. Pidyon-haben (redemption of a firstborn son)

   b. Purification of a mother after childbirth

   The redeeming of the firstborn male reminds the Jewish people of their redemption from slavery in Egypt (Exod. 13) and avoiding the last of the ten plagues to afflict Egypt, namely the death of the firstborn sons, by slaughtering a lamb and putting the blood around their doors.

   As a result, each family dedicates its firstborn son to God's service but then redeems the boy for a payment of five sanctuary shekels (Num. 18:16). This takes place after the son is 30 days old (Num. 3:14).

   Verse 22 suggests either that Mary and Joseph went up to Jerusalem at the time of Pidyon-haben (the redemption of the firstborn male) and remained there 10 days until it was time for Mary's purification, or that they had delayed this observance until the purification.

   The second of these two points of Jewish law was purification of a mother after childbirth as described in

Lev. 12:1-8. The mother of a son remains ceremonially unclean for 40 days after childbirth. On the 41st day a sacrifice is offered. Verse 24 let's us know that Mary and Joseph were poor.

Today, Jewish mothers cannot offer a sacrifice, but they immerse themselves in the Mikvah (baptismal tank) in partial observance of the purification rite.

Today some Orthodox Jewish men immerse themselves in a Mikveh on Friday afternoon in order to be ritually pure before the commencement of Shabbat.[10]

5. In Luke 2:42-50, we read about a 12-year-old Jesus in the temple in what some believe to be an early form of the Bar Mitzvah celebration, Luke 2:42-50. (The Bar Mitzvah became a major life event starting in the Middle Ages). There, Jesus was obligated to live by the Torah of Israel, to keep its commandments and to fulfill the will of God revealed in it (Matt. 5:17).

Today, at the age of 13, a Jewish boy will undergo his Bar Mitzvah in which he becomes a "son of the commandment" now personally responsible for keeping the Torah. He becomes a man in the religious sense. He makes his first *aliyah* (going-up) to the *Bimah* (lectern) and reads from the *Sefer-Torah* (Torah Scroll).

In verses 46-47 of Luke 2 we find Jesus asking questions. This questioning, or what is called *"putting sh'eilot"*

---

10 David H. Stern, *Jewish New Testament Commentary* (Clarksville, MD: Jewish New Testament Publications, 1992), 108-109

or "given to questions" was not one-sided but an intense intellectual dialogue. The scholars were astounded by this boy from Nazareth.

6. Young Jewish boys learned how to read and write by using the Old Testament Scriptures in schools associated with the synagogues.

7. They also learned how to pray there in these schools and learned the history of Israel and traditional interpretation and application of the Scriptures called the "Oral Torah."

8. Jesus being a teacher in the synagogue and in the public was called Rabbi.

9. The Sermon on the Mount reflects the teaching methods of the established teachers of the Talmud.[11]

10. The parables of Jesus have many similarities with the rabbinic teaching tradition[12] and the Lord's Prayer was rabbinical in nature.[13]

11. Jesus would have worn tassels on the four corners of his outer garment called "Tzitzit" (Num. 15:37-41; Deut.

---

11 *The Universal Jewish Encyclopedia,* Vol. 8, "Parallels between the Gospels and Jewish Teachings," 390-393; Robert A. Guelich, *The Sermon on the Mount* (Waco, TX: Word Books, 1982), 329-332

12 Wilson, *Our Father Abraham,* 120

13 Bradford H. Young, *The Jewish Background to the Lord's Prayer* (Austin, TX: Center for Judaic-Christian Studies, 1984); Samuel Sandmel, *Judaism & Christian Beginnings* (New York: Oxford University Press, 1978), 358

22:12). These tassels were also called "wings." The woman said, "If only I may touch His garment (Hem), I shall be made well" (Matt. 9:21). The hem was the tassel. Why did she desire to touch the Hem or Wing? Malachi 4:2 states that the Messiah will come "with healing in His wings."

12. Jesus would have worn *t'fillin* or phylacteries at daily prayer (Deut. 6:4-8). The t'fillin are the little boxes with straps attached and put around the forehead and left arm of the observant Jew. Inside the box is a tiny scroll of the Deuteronomy 6 text.

13. Jesus observed in Jerusalem the great pilgrimage festivals such as Passover (Mark 14:12-25); Shavuot (Feast of Weeks, Pentecost, Firstfruits); Sukkoth (John 7:1-39); Chanukah (Feast of Dedication, John 10:22,23; Dan. 8:13,14)

14. He would have been Kosher, observing the dietary laws

15. After healing the leper, Jesus directed him to "offer the gift (sacrifice) that Moses commanded" and to present himself to the priests to substantiate his healing. (Matt. 8:3,4)

16. The Lord's primary ministry was to Israel, to the Jewish people (Matt. 10:5, 6). However, Jesus' ministry also included non-Jewish people.

Therefore, Jesus and those who followed Him, thought, spoke and acted within a Jewish cultural paradigm.

A Jewish Framework

You will not find within the Lord's teaching a church that is severed from the seed of Abraham. He never envisioned a body that deprecated the Jewish roots. Jesus and his first followers thought and spoke within a Jewish framework. The synoptic Gospels contain no evidence that Jesus visualized a Church which would grow separate from God's chosen people of Israel.[14]

It would be good for us to remember that it was through Abraham's seed that the Messiah came. That the world would not know about God and His Salvation through His Son if it were not for the Jewish messengers who took the gospel to the nations. Jesus said it this way: "Salvation (Heb. *Yeshua*) is from the Jews" (John 4:22 NIV).

Christianity is Jewish

How can we change the unfortunate negative emphasis of Marcionism? Simply, we need to remember, that not only is Jesus Jewish, but Christianity is Jewish.

Ron Moseley, in his book *Yeshua, A Guide to the Real Jesus and the Original Church*, stated: "Contrary to what some believe, the first fifteen bishops of the original Church at Jerusalem were Jewish."[15]

---

14 G.A.F. Knight, *A Biblical Approach to the Doctrine of the Trinity* (Edinburgh: Oliver & Boyd, 1953), 2

15 Ron Moseley, *Yeshua: A Guide to the Real Jesus and the Original Church* (Hagerstown, MD: Ebed Publications, 1996), 1

James, Jesus's half-brother, was the first pastor at the Jerusalem church.

Eusebius, the first church historian, records for us in his work, Ecclesiastical History, Book IV, chapter V, that the first 15 Bishops of the original church were Jewish. And in fact, according to Mosely, evidence shows that all 15 were relatives of Jesus and chosen because of their godly credibility. He lists their names: (1) James; (2) Simeon (some believe was a cousin of the Lord); (3) Justus; (4) Zaccheus; (5) Tobias; (6) Benjamin; (7) John; (8) Matthew; (9) Philip; (10) Seneca; (11) Justus; (12) Levi; (13) Ephres; (14) Joseph; (15) Jude. This dates us to AD 132-135 around the time of the Bar Kochba Revolt.[16]

500 Synagogues

In the first century, it is estimated that there were nearly 500 synagogues in Jerusalem, one being located within the area of the Temple. The early church would have emulated the synagogue in organization. This would have been the model Paul used as he established congregations throughout the Mediterranean area.

Canon

The church owes a debt to the synagogue in many areas:

---

16 Ibid.

The church is a debtor to the Synagogue for the idea of "canon," the concept of sacred authoritative Scripture to rule and guide in all areas of one's life. In the early synagogue, the Scripture was employed in four ways each of which has its counterpart in Christianity.[17]

A. It was read (seder, haftorah)

B. It was expounded (preached, homilies, Midrash)

    Jesus "taught them as one having authority, and not as the scribes." (Matt. 7:29)

C. Translated and paraphrased in the common language (Targums)

    In Nehemiah 8 when Ezra reads the Law, the people stand out of respect and awe. In that state of reverence, they worship God, the God of the Bible. While the people stood in reverence, there were men who translated and paraphrased for the people to "help them understand the reading." They had just returned from 70 years of captivity in Babylon, and many did not understand Hebrew. Therefore, you have the necessity of translators. The people wept when they heard the words of the Law…

D. Scripture was also used in traditional prayers or liturgy.

Other significant ways that the church is a debtor to the

---

17 Daniel Patte, *Early Jewish Hermeneutic in Palestine* (Missoula, MT: Scholars Press, 1975), 35

synagogue include:

A. Emphasis on study and interpreting Scripture was derived from the synagogue.

B. The concept of how to worship came from the synagogue.

C. The idea of the Altar came from Jewish roots.

D. Pulpit (Hebrew: Bimah, Almemar)

E. Titles of church offices

   1. President (Hebrew: Nasi) or the Pastor, Shepherd, Elder, Bishop (rabbi or teacher); the main leader; administrators of the synagogue. Justin Martyr makes reference of this office in 150 AD. Three would form a tribunal to judge cases concerning various issues within the community of believers.

   The Presidents were also known as the "rulers of the synagogue." Jesus mentioned them in Mark 5:3 and Luke 8:41. Paul spoke of their existence in the Gentile Corinthian church in 1 Corinthians 6:1,2.

   2. Chazen (general minister, cantor) who prayed and chose seven people to read from the scriptures each week. He had general oversight of the reading of the Word and congregational responsibilities as well as leading in the worship and

singing.

3. Almoners or parnasin (scholars of the Scriptures, and therefore teachers) cared for the poor and distributed monies, foodstuff, clothing etc., they were the providers or supporters of the congregation. These came to be known as the deacons.

F. The vocabulary of prayer (Amen, Hallelujah) came from the synagogue.

G. Baptism (mikveh, ritual bathing) or "self" immersion came from the synagogue.[18]

H. The Lord's supper (Passover meal which commemorated redemption) came from the Jewish tradition.

Heritage

To properly understand Christian faith is to discover the rich heritage and clear understanding of the Jewish construct that birthed the second of the three monotheistic religions (Judaism, Christianity, and Islam).

Historically, when this happens, there is reformation. One of the by-products of the Reformation in the 16th century was not only the emphasis of "Sola Scriptura" (Scripture

---

[18] David Daube, *The New Testament & Rabbinic Judaism* (London: Athlone Press, 1956), 106-140; David Bivin & Roy Blizzard Jr., *Understanding the Difficult Words of Jesus* (Austin, TX: Center for Judaic-Christian Studies, 1984), 133-137; William S. LaSor, "Discovering What Jewish Mgva'ot Can Tell Us About Christian Baptism," *Biblical Archaeology Review* 13, no. 1, (1987), 55-59

alone as the only and final authority of the believer, over and above tradition), but a renewal and understanding of the Hebraic Roots of Christianity which lasted for approximately two centuries.

The Christian, through Christ, has been made part of the spiritual seed of Abraham (Galatians 3:26-29). Both Jews and Gentiles, who have trusted in Jesus, become children of God. Having immersed themselves into Messiah Jesus by faith, both Jews and Gentiles are equal creating a new community in the Messiah called the Church.

Worship

They are declared righteous by God without the necessity of practicing any particular Jewish or Gentile culturally distinctive forms of worship. If a Jew desires to worship in a Gentile-style congregation, he or she has the freedom to do so. If a Gentile desires to worship in a Messianic-style of congregation, he or she has the freedom to do so.

Unity and fellowship must be encouraged and nurtured between Jew and Gentile, for those who believe in the death, burial and resurrection of Jesus the Messiah are part of the Body of Christ, a new community of faith.

Jewish Roots

The Church, or the Body of Christ, is comprised of both Jewish and Gentile believers. The history of Christianity is birthed and nurtured in her formative years within a Jewish construct. Today's Christian community must never forget their Jewish roots. They must also endeavor to grasp a proper understanding of the faith and religion Jesus founded and to rediscover His Jewish context.

The Bible is a Jewish book, about Jewish prophets, priests, and kings. It speaks of a Jewish Messiah, who sacrificed and shed his blood for the remission of sin and will one day rule the world within the construct of a Jewish Kingdom, from the city of Jerusalem, Israel. Christianity is Jewish!

Bibliography

Barclay, William. *Ethics in a Permissive Society.* New York: Harper & Row, 1971: 13-14.

Biven, David and Roy Blizzard Jr. *Understanding the Difficult Words of Jesus.* Austin, TX: Center for Judaic-Christian Studies, 1984: 73, 133-137, 144-145.

Brunner, Emil, "The Significance of the Old Testament for Our Faith," *The Old Testament & Christian Faith: A Theological Discussion.* Edited by Bernhard W. Anderson. New York: Herder & Herder, 1969: 242.

Daube, David. *The New Testament & Rabbinic Judaism.* London: Athlone Press, 1956: 106-140.

Feingold, Henry L. "The Jewish Role in Shaping American Society," *Time to Speak: The Evangelical-Jewish Encounter.* Edited by A. James Rudin and Marvin R. Wilson. Grand Rapids: William B. Eerdmans Publishing Co., 1987.

Feldman, Abraham J. *Contributions of Judaism to Modern Society.* New York: The Union of American Hebrew Congregations, nd: 5.

Fisher, Eugene J. *Faith without Prejudice*. New York: Paulist Press, 1977: 33.

Guelich, Robert A. *The Sermon on the Mount*. Waco, TX: Word Books, 1982: 329-332.

Heschel, Abraham J. *The Insecurity of Freedom*. New York: Schocken Books, 1972: 169.

Hughes, R. Kent. *Romans: Righteousness from Heaven*. Wheaton, IL: Crossway Books, 1991.

Knight, G.A.F. *A Biblical Approach to the Doctrine of the Trinity*. Edinburgh: Oliver & Boyd, 1953: 2.

LaSor, William S. "Discovering What Jewish Migva'ot Can Tell Us about Christian Baptism," *Biblical Archaeology Review* 13, no. 1, 1987: 55-59.

Moseley, Ron. *Yeshua: A Guide to the Real Jesus and the Original Church*. Hagerstown, MD: Ebed Publications, 1996.

Patte, Daniel. *Early Jewish Hermeneutic in Palestine*. Missoula, MT: Scholars Press, 1975: 35.

Rosovsky, Nitza. *The Jewish Experience at Harvard & Radcliffe*. Cambridge: Harvard University Press, 1986: 2,4,5.

Sandmel, Samuel. *Judaism & Christian Beginnings*. New York: Oxford University Press, 1978: 358.

Stern, David H. *Jewish New Testament Commentary*, Clarksville, MD: Jewish New Testament Publications, 1992.

The Universal Jewish Encyclopedia, Vol. 8. "Parallels between the Gospels and Jewish Teachings": 390-393.

Wilson, Marvin R. *Our Father Abraham: Jewish Roots of the Christian Faith*. Grand Rapids: Eerdmans Publishing Co., 1989: 46, 107-111, 120.

Young, Bradford H. *The Jewish Background to the Lord's Prayer*. Austin, TX: Center for Judaic-Christian Studies, 1984.

About the Author

Dr. Jeffrey Johnson is a dedicated expositor and Bible teacher with expertise in Jewish roots of Christianity, the Middle East, and theology. Dr. Jeff is the founder and president of Israel Today Ministries. He's a teacher, pastor, religious writer, adjunct professor, and  humanitarian feeding thousands in the Middle East. His books and articles address the Jewish roots of Christianity, biblical prophecy, theology, and adventure.

Dr. Jeff has an intense love for Israel and her Messiah. He is motivated by intellectual curiosity, devotion to historic biblical truth, and spiritual awareness. He passionately emphasizes, "As you bless one child, it is as though you are blessing Messiah himself" (Matthew 25:40; Proverbs 14:21).

Dr. Jeff has taught scripture in hundreds of churches and

conferences throughout the United States, Europe, Middle East and Asia. He has also been a visiting professor/speaker at:

> Harvard University
> Greek Bible Institute (Athens, Greece)
> Ariel Ministries
> Arizona College of the Bible
> MJAA Dallas Conference
> IMI Bible Conferences
> Southwestern Baptist Seminary
> Massillon Baptist College
> Arlington Baptist College
> Louisiana Baptist University
> Tennessee Temple University
> International Christian Embassy, Jerusalem

He is simply known as Doctor Jeff: an easy going yet dynamic speaker who can break down the Word of God into its most basic principles with excitement and enthusiasm enough to peak your interest and keep you coming back for more.

Connect with the Author

Israel Today Ministries • Arlington, Texas
www.israeltodayministries.org
Facebook.com/IsraelTodayMinistries
Twitter: @DrJeffITM

Comments from Christian Leaders:

Has for many years faithfully preached the Word of God with accuracy and insight...an able expositor of the Word of God — **John Walvoord, Dallas Theological Seminary**

A careful expositor of Scripture who has a particular interest in prophecy and Jewish studies — **Homer Kent, Grace College and Seminary**

A practitioner of all that he preaches — **Paige Patterson, Southwestern Baptist Theological Seminary**

I heartily recommend Jeffrey Johnson and his ministry — **Edgar C. James, Moody Bible Institute**

The International Christian Embassy Jerusalem has worked with Israel Today Ministries for many years and acknowledges the support in particular that this organization has given to the less privileged and needy in Israel. We are honoured and proud to be working with Israel Today Ministries and have no hesitation in recommending them to other interested groups, individuals and organizations — **Malcolm Hedding, Executive Director, International Christian Embassy Jerusalem**

His commitments to the biblical Word and the "Word made flesh" are processed through his commitment to bringing Jewish studies to bear on both. — **Jeffrey L. Seif, University Distinguished Professor of Bible and Jewish Studies, Kings University**

I warmly recommend Jeffrey D. Johnson as a Bible Expositor with special insights on the origin, nature and destiny of God's chosen people, Israel. — **John C. Whitcomb, Bible Scholar, Author**

I commend and recommend with great enthusiasm the ministry of Jeffrey Johnson. He has a gifted teaching ministry which encompasses Biblical prophecy and insights into modern-day Judaism. — **Paul Tassell, Bible Scholar, Author, Former National Representative of the G.A.R.B.C.**

Thank you for feeding me!